Must L♥VE™ SHOES

*a collection of stories about life
in a woman's shoes*

Julie Gaver

Ruby Slipper Publishers
A division of Julie Gaver Training and Development, LLC

P.O. Box 51
Myersville, MD 21773

Cover Design and Layout by Heather Bodnar
Editing by Anne Rich

ISBN: 978-0-578-04339-5

Table of Contents

To Dan

the yin to my yang

To Craig and Kevin

"I'll love you forever"

I have a genetic penchant for loving shoes. I call it genetic because, in my mind, there is no other logical explanation why we women could own so many of an item when men require only one or two. My friend has a special closet just for her shoes. It has separate pull-out trays which allow her to arrange her prized possessions not only by color, but also by shoe type. Her husband built it for her, which is evidence that this man is highly evolved and truly does understand "what women want."

My friend has an amazing collection of shoes—so much so that when I first saw her collection neatly arranged in this special shoe closet, I felt shoe envy.

Forget the fact that envy is considered one of the seven deadly sins. It doesn't apply to shoe envy. I unapologetically covet her amazing closet and its contents. The day my friend whipped open those double doors to reveal her prized collection, I wept for joy.

One day she finally shared her secret with me: Zappos.com. How could I have been deprived of peep toe pump nirvana for so long? You can find just about any kind of footwear to suit any whimsy or mood imaginable. My husband, whom I shall affectionately refer to as the Shoe Nazi, would *never* approve of this site, and so I have found it necessary to keep this wonderful discovery just between us girls. If he walks into the room to find me lusting at the computer screen... click! When he leaves... click! And so it continues each time he enters and exits my office. I do believe he is becoming suspicious. Certainly some day I will read a letter in *Dear Abby* from a distraught husband who is convinced that his wife is either addicted to internet porn or having an on-line affair when it's really just me, having a little shoe orgy of my own!

There are certain things that only women understand, like how finding the perfect pair of heels can totally change your attitude when you walk. Or why we need to have ten variations of black pants to match every possible combination of mood and weight. Or how sometimes we don't need someone else to fix our problems but rather just someone who won't add to them. Men don't always get that, do they?

As I age, I have come to value my relationships with the women in my life even more. Men may come and go. Children grow up and leave the nest, but your girlfriends are with you forever. I am convinced that we need to do a better job staying connected with other women—women who inspire, challenge, understand, care about, and more importantly, love us for who we are. And so, I'm recruiting you, my dear reader, to be one of *my girls*. The criteria for this job are quite simple. You must love life. You must love to laugh. You must not take yourself too seriously.

And… you must love shoes! Welcome to my sisterhood!

I have a confession to make! I do not weigh what my
driver's license claims. It's not even close! I was tired of
living a lie, and so this past year I righted a thirty-year
wrong. When the young, 20-something disengaged Motor
Vehicle Administration employee stared at her computer
screen and asked if there were any changes to be made, I
proudly blurted out my REAL weight! It was exhilarating!
I felt free! I felt liberated! Surely she would applaud the
great strides I had made to accept myself unconditionally!

Nothing. No response. No comment. No change of
expression. At the very least she could have lied and said I
didn't look it, but noooooo. She just stared at the screen
and typed. (If I am ever contracted to provide customer
service training to the DMV you can bet that I'm going to
address the important art of sucking up to the customer!)

She then instructed me to stand in front of the camera.
Perhaps it was the afterglow from my newfound acceptance.
Who knows? But when I retrieved the final product, I
laughed out loud. It is the BEST picture I have ever taken.
Olan Mills couldn't have done better! Surely the next time
I'm stopped for speeding, the officer will praise me for
being so photogenic. It was as if the universe was sending

the karma and rewarded me by saying "You go, girl."

My friend, Sherry, had a different DMV experience. At age 16 she weighed in at a svelte 115 pounds. Now, she's a *gorgeous* cougar-aged curvy girl. At one license renewal session, the clerk asked Sherry her weight. Realizing that, 35 years later, it had been quite a while since she saw 115 on the scale, Sherry asked, "Do I have to put my *real* weight on there?" The very kind lady (*obviously part of our 'sisterhood'*) replied, "Honey, have you ever seen a state trooper with a set of scales in the back seat?" And so, Sherry (who is in her 50's) still weighs 115 pounds… on her driver's license! As they say, "Sometimes fiction is greater than truth." Or is it the other way around?

I do care about health and fitness. I have to because it seems that everyone around me has become an exercise addict. My sons run, my husband runs, my friends run, and I... try. But if the entire time you are running you are fantasizing about vegging on the sofa watching reruns of *Sex in the City*, you're in no danger of becoming an addict.

I can't run without an endless supply of comfort enhancers and external stimulation. While on the treadmill, I utilize three forms of artificial coolant: central air, a window fan, and the treadmill fan, turned on high. I am still hot and not in that good, sexy, way!

The TV plays the Food Channel Network and I watch Giada De Laurentiis serve up pasta to die for! (Does running while watching new ways to prepare carbs constitute an oxymoron?)

My iPod produces the final critical distraction and is key to keeping me engaged and entertained. But I wonder what my friends at church would think if they knew that I was running to the likes of Sir Mix-a-Lot's "Baby Got Back"!

At some point during each of the runs, I have an epiphany:

the good thing about back fat is that, unless you are masochistic and consciously look, you don't even know it's back there. Ignorance quickly becomes bliss. Seriously, if God intended for us to see the state of our backsides on a regular basis, he would have given us eyes in the back of our head!

I dream of the day when I read the following review of one of my presentations."… and the audience was so spellbound by Ms. Gaver's inspiring message that they failed to notice that when the air conditioner kicked on, her underarms began floating gently in the breeze." Enough! Now, where IS that pasta??????

I was a cheerleader in high school. Before you dismiss me by conjuring up images of today's navel-baring, cleavage-toting professional cheerleaders (*I'm sorry, public relations spokeswomen*), let me just say that *high school* cheerleading in the early to mid-seventies was, in my very humble opinion, an athletic sport. If you don't believe me, try doing a backwards flip or leap high into the air so that when you land (without resistance) you end in a split. Ouch! (Trust me… if I tried that now, there would be serious gynecological consequences!)

In my youth, cheerleading provided an appropriate outlet for the innate perkiness that, to this day, continues to well up inside me. You could wear smiley face buttons, garish colors like bright orange and black, and other random motivational accessories in the name of school spirit—all without alerting the fashion police.

My P.E. teacher did not like cheerleaders. Perhaps she did not agree with my interpretation of it being a sport. She called any of us who could successfully perform a syncopated stomp-clap a bunch of "simpletons, simple girls, or sissies." Had I been able to execute a proper flick or block tackle during our field hockey unit, I surely would have redeemed myself in her eyes, but, unfortunately, my athletic prowess was limited to the stomp-clap.

I'd like to formally go on record saying that, in my adult life, I've never been thrown out of any public institution for disturbing the peace. I did, however, get thrown out of gym class once for disturbing girl's intramural basketball. Apparently my practice stomp-clapping from the sidelines was *louder* than the six basketball games (complete with bouncing balls, screaming girls, and whistle blowing) happening on the courts. (I'm *still* bitter). The one thing I *did* learn from that experience was that when *anyone* sporting a whistle continually gives you the stink eye, there's a good chance that you will be removed from the premises.

Fast forward twenty years. After that, I was *totally* not athletic (surprise!!) but decided to coordinate my office's fundraising team for the Arthritis Foundation's Jingle Bell *Run*. I coerced my husband and two young sons into running alongside me because I was seriously thinking I would need moral support to prevent horrible gym class flashbacks. In addition to raising monies for this cause, my goal for that race was twofold and quite simple: to finish and not be last! How hard could that be? Besides, it was only a 5K race!

Well, let me tell you something about the opposite sex, if you haven't already figured this one out! They talk a big talk about being there for you, but the moment they sniff something that even *remotely* smells like competition, the testosterone kicks in and all bets are off! I quickly found myself *alone*.

Here's a hint should you ever decide to run in a race of any kind: if you never look back, you won't know you're last. Unfortunately, I had to learn that little nugget the hard way. Let's just say that if I wasn't last, I was so far ahead, I couldn't see my followers. That was not likely the case. I turned back around, feeling defeated although vowing to hold my head high and yuck it up for the crowd should I be the last one across the finish line.

Suddenly, the unthinkable happened! As I heard the pitter patter of feet quickly approaching from behind, I heard a voice that, to this day, forever haunts me.

"Come OOOOONNNNN, Kuhn. Pick 'em up! Pick 'em up!" (*Kuhn was my maiden name.*) As if shifting from third to first gear, the figure who sprinted by me was none other than… than… Miss Stink Eye! Miss No-Stomp-Clapping-In-My-Gym! Little Miss "You're-a-Simpleton. Miss I-AM-IN-MY-

SEVENTIES-NOW-AND-CAN-*STILL*-BEAT-YOUR YOUNG BUTT!!!!!

She passed me in such a blur that you would have thought the grand prize was a free year's membership to AARP! I was humiliated! Now, in my mind instead of people cheering encouragingly for my fortitude and perseverance when I crossed the finish line *last*, I imagined they would all be holding their fingers to their forehead in the oh-so-horrible-LOSER-sign! And so... I SPRINTED. Think Chariots of Fire. Think Florence Griffith-Joyner. Think football player intercepting the pass and running 60 yards for a tie-breaking touchdown! *Run, Julie, Run!*

If I were writing fiction, this is the point in the story when I would write that I broke some kind of record because, for the first time in my young, impressionable life, I believed in myself, saw myself as a winner... blah blah blah. But this is not fiction. Ladies, I'm here to tell you the rest of the story:

I finished.

I was *not* last! (surprise)

I helped to raise a lot of money for a very good cause...

and

My 70's something PE teacher won first place in her age bracket. (*Perhaps there's still hope for me!*)

And I can still do an impressive stomp-clap!

Naughty but Nice

*M*y friend Deb's two-year-old granddaughter gets sent to the "naughty mat" whenever she is bad or needs to contemplate her actions. Although I'm an adult, there have definitely been times when my behavior merited a visit to the naughty mat. I often say or do things that, in retrospect, I realize just shouldn't have happened.

A plethora of wardrobe malfunctions have haunted me during my professional career. In a previous life I worked in Marketing and Public Relations for a CPA firm. The dress code was professional yet in my opinion, a tad conservative. Although I followed the rules, the inner "naughty girl" in me rebelled against the thought of spending what felt like an eternity in navy blue pinstripe and pantyhose. (*There is **no** way I will ever believe that pantyhose were invented by a woman, but I digress.*) A quick trip to Victoria's Secret fixed that problem! One July morning I walked into the office wearing my "I have a mind for business" attire, but I was sporting a pair of sexy, seductive thigh-high stockings underneath. Actually, I didn't *walk* into that office, I *slithered* like a true naughty girl. I felt sexy and savored the fact that my body imprisoned by pantyhose for so long finally felt *free*! I looked the part on the outside but definitely had a little secret going on. No one was the wiser.

I learned a lot about thigh-high stockings that day. They are not meant for long term wear, at least not for naughty girls with "healthy" thighs. As the day progressed, my exhilaration over my private act of defiance waned. When I stood after being seated for a while, slight slippage occurred. By lunchtime it was much more pronounced. By late afternoon, let's just say the uber-elastic was definitely feeling the strain. I could not wait until 5:00 as I spent the final hours confined to my desk in fear of lingerie abandonment.

Finally, the moment of truth arrived. I had survived the ordeal only to find that my walk to the car would go down in history as one of my most embarrassing moments. Halfway across the long, heavily populated parking lot, my stockings screamed "UNCLE" and made their slow agonizing descent to my ankles. I entered the building that morning looking on the exterior like the poster child for the latest edition of "Dress for Success" and exited looking like my grandmother who intentionally rolls her hose to her mid calf.

Little did I know at the time that it would not be the last time my undergarments would render me speechless.

＊＊＊＊＊＊＊＊＊＊＊＊＊＊＊＊

It's
So Easy

I have a home-based business. The good news is that it brings new meaning to the term Casual Day. The *bad* news is that it brings new meaning to the term Casual Day. If I am not scheduled to speak on a given day, it is likely that I am working at my desk in plaid flannel pj's and thermal under-wear. If I'm feeling particularly adventurous, I don't even brush my teeth until I leave the house! I don't use SKYPE and other video conferencing tools, and it's not because I am a techie illiterate. I am merely protecting my right to be… well… casual. In spite of what you read in the last chapter, I do spend a respectable amount of time looking professional when I'm in public.

But I do love Fridays because Friday is errand day. I certainly don't run errands in my pj's but I do have the luxury of being a little more informal than usual. Friday is the day that I perform all the duties I would not have to do if I had an assistant… banking, post office, and the weekly trek to Staples.

I adore Staples, mostly because the one I frequent has an employee who truly understands good customer service. His name is Robert. One day Robert greeted me upon entering the store. When I finally made my way to his checkout line a half hour later, he replied, "THERE you are!"

"Oh. Have you been waiting for me?" I asked.

"I've been waiting for you my entire life," he playfully replied.

I know a schmoozer when I see one, but when someone has so skillfully mastered the fine art of sucking up, you just can't help but be impressed. I'll admit it, Robert helped make Staples my favorite stop on errand day.

One Friday, after a particularly hectic week of training, I woke up joyfully realizing that it was errand day. No make-up? Check! Hair in a scrunchie (no judging!)? Check! Do I dare wear the jeans that were haphazardly thrown on the floor from a few days ago? Check-a-roonie! Off to the post office I go. On to the bank. Final destination: Staples. YAY! Up and down the aisles I shop until I find myself in line waiting to once again experience Robert's unique brand of humor.

I will readily admit that I am not the most observant member of the female species but, as I stood in line, I sensed that something just wasn't right. Upon glancing down at the floor, I realized that I had dragged Casual Day down to an all-time low. There hanging out of the bottom of my jeans was a pair of previously worn black bikini underwear!

What exactly does a lady do when she realizes that strangers are now privy to her personal tastes in panties? How much attention would I draw to myself if I conducted the search and rescue mission needed to save the lingering lingerie? Heck! Panties are expensive. I can't afford to take a chance on losing the wayward undergarments altogether!

So I did what any self-respecting, proper woman would do. I bent over, fetched those suckers right up, stuffed them in my pocket with all the dignity I could muster… and acted like nothing… ever… happened.

I would had been successful, too, had it not been for the man who was standing next to me in line. He glanced down at my feet and looked me in the eye with a smirk on his face.

"Niiiiiiice," he said.

* * * * * * * * * * * * * * * *

How to Meet
New People

I guess by now you are thinking there is not a lot of gray matter in this brain of mine. In my defense, the problem is not that I don't think. The problem is that I am so easily distracted.

As I mentioned before, Friday is always Errand Day for my home-based business. One such Friday, my husband took a day off from work and came up with the novel idea that we would spend time together. In order to make that happen, it was necessary that he accompany me on my weekly pilgrimage to Errand Land.

The trek to the post office was without incident. My visit to the bank, however, was another story. My husband drove, and as he pulled into the bank parking lot, I said, "I'll only be a *minute*." He decided to just wait for me in the car.

Who was I kidding???? I'll only be a minute??? Sometimes I wonder why words like that even come out of my mouth when I know that if there are people present, there is opportunity for conversation, and I've NEVER taken just one minute for conversation!

As luck would have it, I ran into my friend Ashley, who

worked at the bank. Let's just say time flew. As we neared the end of our conversation, I remembered that I was not alone.

I pictured my husband, Dan, in the car, assuming "the position." (Assuming the position refers to the fact that his body language clearly indicates when he thinks it is time for me to SHUT UP so we can go home. At church, I KNOW I'm in trouble when he positions himself by the door with his arms crossed, sporting the same [lack of] facial expression as the guards outside of Buckingham Palace in London.)

As I mentioned earlier, I'm easily distracted. When I realized that a *significant* amount of time had lapsed since uttering the words "I'll only be a minute," I hurriedly said goodbye to my friend and ran out the bank and across the parking lot. (Truthfully, I think the only reason I ran was so that if Dan happened to be looking in the rear view mirror *at that exact moment*, he would see that I was actually trying to hurry.)

As I approached the passenger's side of the car, I grabbed the door handle and hurled myself into the idling vehicle. As my keister hit the seat, I simultaneously turned to my husband to begin my apologies.

Suddenly I realized that I was... sitting… in… the… wrong… car!

What I'm about to tell you next must always stay just among us for fear that, if it got out, I'll be checking into assisted living by the weekend.

The car that I was sitting in was not even the same COLOR as my husband's!

There was a man sitting behind the wheel (also obviously waiting "for just a minute.") He turned to look at me in horror. At the moment our eyes locked, realizing that we were NOT each other's betrothed, I said, "Heeeeeelllllllll-llo."

As if there was ever any doubt, I can assure you that there is no danger of me ever becoming a street hooker because jumping into a strange man's car just felt *wrong* on so many levels! (And by the look of confusion and *fear* in the poor man's eyes, he was obviously already formulating HIS take on why a strange woman was sitting in his car, in case his wife returned.)

Have you ever noticed that when something strange

happens to you, it feels like the events are occurring in slow motion? It's like a movie where the process of slowing down the film causes the voices to sound several octaves lower, Darth Vader-like! The last memory I have of the rather unfortunate situation was the memory of not only this poor, befuddled man's face, but also the view of Dan looking over at me from the next car. Now THAT, my friends, was a Kodak moment!

Blonde
Ambition

Several years ago, my husband and I took on a major redecoration and renovation of our 150-year-old home. In the 28 years that we've lived in the house, we've never done so much work in one grand swoop. It was stressful but at the same time quite fun.

Did I mention that I'm addicted not only to the Food Channel Network, but also to HGTV? (Exactly how does one get selected to have Candace Olson or David Bronson redesign your home? Sign me up!)

One of the many projects involved redecorating a small powder room on the first floor. During my planning, I discovered this super cute mirror in a home & garden magazine that I thought I just *had* to find for this room. The mirror had no frame, beveled edges, and an octagonal shape. Instead of attaching it to the wall in a customary fashion, it was hung by a decorative ribbon on an ornate, antique-looking knob. I *had* to have it! Like an explorer in search of new land, I scoured the local home décor establishments in my area. Unfortunately, I had disappointing luck at first.

Finally, I found it! I was thrilled! Overjoyed! Surely this was the closest I would ever come to the jubilation HGTV home-owners must feel when they are accessory shopping for their made-for-TV home makeover.

The picture on the box of the mirror showed it hanging on a wall with the exact ribbon and knob that I mentioned, so my next agenda item was to find that knob.

The bigger the store, the more challenging the hunt, and this was no exception. When I finally found the appropriate aisle, I was disappointed to find no adorable ornate, antique-looking candidates. This prompted my search for a highly motivated, superior customer service-oriented, 'I-love-my-job-and-I'm-here-to-serve-you' employee. I know… what planet am I from????

Out of respect, I won't tell you the store's name, but let's just say the employee whose assistance I sought was wearing an orange apron! I explained my dilemma to him. *"I saw this mirror in a magazine… had to have it… it will look adorable in my new powder room. I found it here. Love the knob. Looked for the knob. Can't find it. I'm disappointed… can you help me?"*

The entire time I relived the dramatic events leading up to

my plea for help, the apron-wearing man stood with his arms crossed with a patronizing expression on his face. He waited until I finished and, without saying a word, reached over and tapped the box. As I glanced down at the box, I noticed the words "hardware included."

"Oh!" I exclaimed, *"I'm so sorry. I didn't see that... that's great. Thanks!"*

He responded, *"Are you sure you're not a blonde?"*

You've *got* to be kidding me!

"Haven't We Met Before?"

I have a hereditary condition I refer to as "Who's yer daddy?" syndrome. Coincidently, I inherited this syndrome from my Dad who can talk to anyone, anytime, anywhere. His primary objective when meeting someone for the first time is to accomplish some kind of connection. "Do you know so-and-so?" "Where did you go to school?" "Are you related to...?" "Didn't I see you last week at...?"

This condition is both a blessing and a curse because it has led me to develop another ailment called "foot in mouth" disease. The fact that my "condition" flares up when I'm in front of an audience makes for some lively training moments.

One such experience happened several years ago while I was giving an inspirational speech to a local women's philanthropy organization. Since it was in my home town, I was excited about the possibility of seeing people I knew because I don't always give presentations on my home turf. I was to be the after lunch speaker so during the meal, I spent my time chatting with the ladies at my table and surveying the room to see who was there! (One of the symptoms of someone with who's-yer-daddy syndrome is that they will spend a disproportionate amount of time talking relative to eating during any communal meal.)

During my survey of the room, I spotted a woman who looked *vaguely* familiar. I readily admit that names often escape me (especially now that I can add menopausal to my long list of afflictions, but that's ANOTHER story), but I *never* forget a face! "Where have I seen her before?" Hmmmmmm… I love a good mystery! Enter Nancy Drew!

Throughout the presentation, in the back of my mind I continued to contemplate this woman's true identity. *Was it my imagination or was she also doing the same?* She smiled. *(I never once thought she was smiling because of my presentation. Surely she's wondering "How do I know her?" as well!—this is typical who's-yer-daddy reasoning).* It was beginning to haunt me. *She looks so familiar. But does she? I dunno, maybe I just want so badly to see someone I know today that I'm imagining all of this!*

Finally, the presentation ended and my favorite part of my job began. People came to the front of the room and began chatting with me about themselves, what they thought of the message, how it related to them, and other stories or experiences they wanted to share. As I stood surrounded by several women enjoying a rousing gab fest, the unknown woman approached me with a smile on her face. I immediately interrupted my conversation and invited her into the fold.

"Have we met before?" I asked immediately. Finally! An end to this mystery! "I'm not sure but you look so familiar," she replied. "There's something about your facial expressions and animation. You seem familiar," she continued.

Shifting into true who's-yer-daddy? mode, I began the cross-examination:

Do you live in the area?
Do you have children in the school system?
Where do you go to church?
Do you come here often?

By this time I realize that it's beginning to sound like a ridiculous blending of cheesy pick-up lines or prisoner of war interrogation tactics but I WILL NOT STOP BEFORE I GET THE ANSWER.

Finally, I asked the most obvious question, which I had neglected to begin with (did I mention I actually TEACH networking skills???)

WHAT IS YOUR NAME?

Upon hearing her response, I then realized that the mystery woman was my new gynecologist!

Now, in my defense, I had recently switched practices and had seen her only once. If I recall, she was wearing a white lab coat with her hair pulled back. She looked quite different standing in front of me at this luncheon. And, for crying out loud, I don't subscribe to the "lean up and WATCH your GYN while they work" philosophy! I've spent MOST of my life trying NOT to run into people who have seen me naked. I never expected to be pursuing one of them.

Who's-yer-daddy has now left the building. Enter foot-in-mouth for Act II.

"OH!!!!" I exclaimed. "YOU'RE MY GYNECOLOGIST!!!"
I blurted loudly.

Thank goodness I had remembered to turn off my lapel microphone.

The other ladies witnessing this interchange laughed hysterically. I'm sure they were thinking, "Better you than me, sweetheart!"

My new doctor (I'm sure she has experienced this often) replied with great tact and grace, "I'm sorry I didn't recognize you. You look *lovely* today."

Lead, Follow, or
Get Out of
my Way!

*T*here has been a significant amount of research collected over the years on the subject of crowd behavior. As a frequent presenter at conferences, I've drawn my own conclusions about the human personality based on what I've observed from the platform.

Several years ago I presented a concurrent session on the topic of humor in the workplace. This is one of my favorite topics, not only because I love to talk about it, but because, invariably, funny things happen during the course of our time together. This conference was no exception.

We were about 45 minutes into the interactive seminar and the audience was getting very lively. The session included some small group activity, participants were sharing hilarious stories, and I was wound up! We were having a blast! There was amazing chemistry between audience and speaker to the point that if I was a contestant on *The Bachelor*, I'd be going home with a rose! Hopefully you get the picture that I was truly *feelin' the love.*

I had reached the point in the presentation when I talk about the importance of taking humor breaks throughout the workday as a strategy for relieving stress and maintaining a positive attitude. I often refer to these breaks as *recess* and challenge the audience members to "reclaim their childhood by taking back recess."

No sooner had the words left my mouth when the fire alarm system at the conference center began to WAIL. As luck would have it, not only was there a speaker in our room, but a strange strobe-like light began to pulsate. The sound was deafening! Like one of Pavlov's dogs, the stimuli produced an immediate flashback to my elementary school days when emergency drills were held periodically, requiring us to scramble under our desks or be herded into the gymnasium in the unlikely event that my small community was subjected to a natural disaster or military strike.

It could have been the flashback, the element of surprise, or even the fact that, at times, I'm a tad overcaffeinated, but I JUMPED and screamed, "WHAT IS THAT???? IS THAT THE FIRE ALARM??????"

The audience laughed! "REALLY????" I screeched, "WHAT"S GOING ON?????" They laughed even harder! They say that three time's a charm, so this time I decided to stop asking these laughing hyenas questions and take matters into my own hands.

I started to leave the stage, stopped, turned around, and started again in utter confusion over what to do. *Do I act like this is not happening and keep on talking?* (I was now having flashbacks to the scene from *Titanic* where the ship is SINKING, people are jumping overboard and the musicians continue to PLAY!!!!!)

Do I take the lead and begin herding these wonderful people outside to safety, fulfilling my lifelong dream of being Wonder Woman, dedicated to saving innocent people from crime and other forms of destruction?

For a nanosecond that sounded appealing in spite of the fact that I readily admit I'm lacking the body to pull off that cleavage-filled Lycra form-fitting blue and red jumpsuit that is obviously critical to performing heroic acts.

By this time the crowd had become so entertained by my legitimate angst that some even pounded the tables in hysteria. Suddenly, I had a revelation! These people are NUTS! They think this is all part of an act!

My only course of action immediately became crystal clear. I ran off the stage, grabbed my purse, ran back onto the stage and screamed, "I DON'T KNOW ABOUT YOU, BUT

I'M OUTTA HERE!" And with that, they applauded.

By the time I was halfway down the aisle towards the back door, a very official looking conference center employee entered the ballroom and asked everyone to exit the building.

As the conference attendees stood outside awaiting authorization to re-enter the building, one woman approached me saying, "Really, will you tell us *now*, how DID you DO that????"

Sometimes, you just get lucky!

Groundhog
Day

Disclaimer: No animals were harmed in the telling of this next story.

*T*he one thing I love more than telling a good story is flower gardening. My backyard is certainly my *happy place.* I take great pride in my hobby and have been known to pluck any poor, unsuspecting soul who happens to pass my house for a spontaneous garden tour.

However, usually in late spring and early summer, I am not happy! Let's just say there is trouble in paradise! If I were to put this in workplace terms, there is major discord between management and staff.

I (*management*) prefer a neat and orderly yard. Staff (*the wildlife who live there*) prefer to run amuck. They have little regard for my feelings and the vision I have for my haven. That angers me.

The squirrels bury nuts in arbitrary places; voles dig holes in my newly mulched flower beds. The neighborhood cat is convinced that eating the goldfish from my pond helps meet her daily protein requirements. The deer consume massive quantities of flora as if it is senior discount night at the Golden Corral!

But the varmint that distresses me most is the groundhog. (For this reason, I defiantly boycott February 2 every year and refuse to watch the movie bearing the title in spite of the fact that I think Bill Murray is a comedic genius!)

In addition to the fact that I find the groundhog's looks repulsive, I also find him disrespectful and destructive. I've tried on countless occasions to live in harmony with the critter, but to no avail. He mocks me! Like a scene from *Caddyshack*, he takes great delight in watching me make a fool of myself as he shows little regard for my authority and position.

Once while mowing the yard, I spotted the groundhog hiding in one of my flower beds. Upon eyeing the uninvited hairy-looking mammal, I immediately made a hard left hand turn and began sprinting across the yard, push mower in tow, towards the bed. This was done in an effort to scare the *bajeebas* out of him. (It's a word – go with it!) It apparently worked. He scurried the length of the fence alongside the outbuilding, and, as I continued in hot pursuit, he scampered across the yard, landing in the flowers that surround my fish pond.

He obviously never heard the rumor about redheads having

a temper because I do believe he thought that was the end of the story. Ohhhhh noooooo, no, no, no, no! Still pushing the lawn mower, I started to run towards the stone pond wall, fully prepared to sacrifice my beloved flowers along the way. *But for what?* There was *no way* I would run *over* him. I can't even stand to watch operating room scenes on *Grey's Anatomy* without covering my eyes. It was as if I actually thought that if I scared him enough, he would bow down right there in the yard and *beg* my forgiveness, promising never to mess with me or my flowers again! By now, I was crazed! Once again, the groundhog shot across the yard with me in hot pursuit until he, unfortunately, made his getaway.

Several days later, I happened to look out my second floor bedroom window to find the little bastard sitting on his hind legs on the patio beneath my window. Was it my imagination, or was he looking up at me in the window, smirking????? How *dare* he taunt me in MY home!!!!

"THIS MEANS WAR!!" I said to myself and to the groundhog. Nobody ridicules me and gets away with it. If guns were allowed (I live in town), I probably would have pulled a Granny from *The Beverly Hillbillies*. Instead, I was forced to go the humanitarian route. Two days later, I captured my enemy and he was transferred to the country. No doubt, today he is somewhere feasting off another poor soul's beautiful yard, telling his backyard cronies about the wild woman who lost her mind over his silly antics.

A Ride on
the Wild Side

*T*here are only two possible reasons why my hubby and I would choose to *drive 18 hours* to Florida with pre-adolescent boys in a minivan: our desire to save money or total insanity! Guilty as charged on both counts!

With an endless supply of handheld video games, snacks, books, and a van filled with optimism, we began our two-day trek to visit my sister for some warm weather fun.

In the beginning, we were the quintessential All-American family on vacation. Everyone was happy and there was good conversation, singing, and an endless supply of travel fun (*alphabet games, see-how-many-state-license-plates-you-can-spot and a host of other wholesome entertainment methods.*) Somewhere along the way, that changed.

The family who was previously happier than the Brady Bunch began to bicker like a bunch of *Real World* reality show contestants.

"Mom, make him quit it!" "Mom, he's *touching* me!" "Mom, I have to go to the bathroom." "Mom, he's *looking* at me!" "If you don't stop *looking* at me, I'm gonna tell." (*As if I hadn't already heard the whining all the way from the back seat! Only in a cranky child's world does looking at someone constitute a criminal offense!)*

Let's just say that after eight hours of this nonsense, the driver on our bus didn't say, "Move on back," but "DON'T *MAKE* ME STOP THIS VAN!!!!!"

When we reached the one-more-hour-of-driving-till-we-look-for-a-hotel mark, Dan announced that he needed a final pit stop for refueling and a cup of java. As the van was in the service bay filling up, he ran inside to grab his caffeine, leaving the bickering boys and me in the van.

Suddenly, we heard the most frightening sound. A car careened off the highway exit, speeding across the Sheetz parking lot, and, with tires squealing, slammed on the brakes landing the vehicle in the service bay immediately next to us. The sight and sound was such a spectacle that all three pairs of eyes were glued to the car to see what might happen next!

A woman with a crazed look in her eye jumped out of the car from behind the wheel. Her apparent husband, looking a tad subdued, was in the front passenger seat. Three *teenagers* sat knee-to-knee in the back seat of the car looking visibly uncomfortable and cramped. The driver slammed her door so hard that the car shook. Stomping to the back window, she stooped over so that she could peer inside the back window displaying her three precious offspring.

Had the next few minutes been videotaped, this country would surely have the perfect ad campaign for future public school sex education programs promoting abstinence. Because no teenager in his or her right mind would ever *dream* of having sex if they thought it could end up like this!

Mommy Dearest began tapping on the back window. The guttural sound coming out of her throat was reminiscent of demons exiting Linda Blair's body in *The Exorcist*!

"I… can't… staaaaaannnd… yooooou!" she growled.

"I can't stand YOOOOOU! *(She tapped on the window at child no. 1.)*

…and YOOOOOU! *(She tapped on the window at child no. 2.)*

and… I… REALLY… don't… like… YOOOOU!!!!" *(She double tapped on the window at child no. 3.)*

And with *that*, she ran into the Sheetz! *(I must confess, in retrospect, that my behavior in our car leading up to witnessing such an eruption now seemed as passive as Carol Brady's in the episode when the Brady kids' antics caused her favorite vase to get broken!)*

Judging by the stark silence in our vehicle, the boys and I were surely traumatized by such a frightening display of drama! Suddenly, from the back of my van came an angelic little voice saying, "Mommy, I think that woman needs a *time out!*"

Some days are like that, aren't they?

Just What
the Doctor
Ordered

I am a huge believer in the therapeutic power of self care. Every woman needs to find ways of putting fuel in her tank. We differ on our preferences as much as we differ on the kind of shoes that make us purr.

Once, while conducting a women's stress reduction workshop, I asked the group to share ways they relieve stress. Many of the responses were similar: exercise, listen to good music, talk to a friend, and so on. One woman's response, however, I will always remember. *"If I get home from work and am feeling stressed, I just grab my car keys, tell my family I'm goin' to High's to get a gallon of milk and I just don't come back!"*

As the class chuckled, she continued, "I just drive around town with the radio cranked up high laughin' to myself about how long it will take till they realize I'm not comin' back and they're not gettin' dinner!" Of course, she always goes back eventually, but a little bit of fantasy can go a long way, can't it, girlfriends? Can I hear an AMEN???

My self care ritual of choice is to treat myself to a European facial every six weeks. A European facial is much more than an ordinary facial. It's better than ANYTHING. Better than finding an article of clothing which makes you look delightfully fabulous, only to realize, when you get to the register, that it is an additional 40% off an already discounted price! It's better than *snowballs*! (If you have never eaten these decadently sweet chocolate with marshmallow filling, pink or white (your choice) coconut-covered cupcakes, well, you just haven't lived. As a matter of fact, it's better than SEX because you can fall asleep halfway through the hour-long experience and not be accused of being insensitive or unresponsive!)

My aesthetician's name is Anna. She is one of the most beautiful women I've ever met because her beauty radiates from the inside out. She has a relaxed and delightfully serene demeanor that I find extremely therapeutic (as do most yoga instructors—have you ever noticed that? I guess that's because they practice what they preach! What a concept.)

If you have never treated yourself this way, you simply must! I'm not exaggerating when I say that the first time I indulged, I felt the earth move and the angels sing. OK not really, but I can tell you that it took every ounce of self control I had to keep from moaning out loud. By the time Anna finishes with me, I feel like "butta."

At some point during each session, Anna extols the virtues of drinking water, the importance of healthy eating (she's a vegetarian… I was one once for a day), and I leave with a renewed commitment to change my bad habits before my next visit.

I'm proud to say that the commitment lasts until I swing by the Dairy Queen, three blocks away, on the drive home. OK, so nobody's perfect.

Fantasy
Island

Every December I receive an annual dose of what it's like to live a charmed life. Among the holiday greeting cards and well wishes is the ever so popular annual holiday letter. In defense of many of my friends, this form of correspondence is an efficient way to keep family and friends apprised of current happenings when regular contact is not possible. But, unfortunately for others, these letters can border on fiction that seems so outlandish I just want to say, "Ricardo Montalban called and they want you back on Fantasy Island." Let's get real. Is anyone's life really THAT perfect? If it is, I vote for keeping it to yourself or at least throwing the rest of us a reality bone so we feel we even stand a chance.

So, I decided to write my own annual holiday letter just for you, dear readers. Consider this the perfectly (REAL) life of Julie Gaver.

Dear Friends and Family,

Happy holidays. I hope this letter finds you and yours happy, healthy, and looking forward to an exciting new year. 2009 has been an eventful year for the Gaver clan.

Craig and Kevin, ages 26 and 23, both have jobs and live on their own. No awards, honors or admission into the most prestigious school can compare to the satisfaction of knowing that we no longer pay for their food or electric bills.

Both of our sons shake hands like they mean it and are kind to elderly people, two qualities I admire in young people today. We are very proud. I'm sad to report, however, that during a recent visit home, I spotted one of the Gaver boys picking a worn shirt off the floor and subjecting it to the smell test before putting it on. I was initially appalled until I remembered that their mother has been known to drag previously worn underpanties around town in the legs of her jeans. I guess the apple doesn't fall far from the tree.

This year Dan and I celebrated 30 years of marriage. Many people ask our secret to this great accomplishment. It is quite simple. As most of you know, Dan is a man of *few* words. This is perfect because I'm a woman of *many*. Seriously, can you imagine thirty years of competing for air time?

In addition, Dan is a list maker. I don't like lists. There

are already too many little voices in my head telling me what to do. So Dan makes lists for everyone. When the boys were home, he made lists for all of us. That ended some time ago which is why we've been married for thirty years.

At the same time, Dan doesn't really need to make lists. He has an impeccable memory. He can recite the exact date, year, and relative time we purchased every vehicle we've ever owned as well as how much we paid. He remembers the anniversary of the purchase of our home and can calculate tax and tip on even the most complicated restaurant tabs. I, on the other hand, can tell you what you were wearing the last time I saw you as well as all of your family's names. Some may say that constitutes a match made in heaven.

This past year I began a self improvement plan which included getting Visalign braces. In preparation for the shifting of crowded teeth, one needed to be removed. You guessed it. They removed the one right in the center. I no longer find humor in those horrid West Virginia jokes.

Once, in the middle of a speech on leadership to a very professional group, my retainer popped out of my mouth, nearly projectile. Lucky for me I played baseball with my brothers in my youth. I caught that sucker before it even had a chance to hit the ground and nonchalantly buried it in my pocket as I continued. I'm very proud to say that I never missed a beat. At the break, I mentioned my embarrassment to one of the class members who replied, "I saw that. I thought you were just spitting out your gum." Well, there you have it! No one ever said I was classy.

My self improvement goals this year have also involved finding a sport that did not make me want to kill something. I found yoga. I'd like to say my motivation is to find inner peace but, in reality, I want to look like I have "tickets to the gun show." The instructor makes us do pretzel-like twisty moves and endless repetitions of a move which has a fancy, spiritual sounding name but is really bad-ass military style push-ups. I am not fooled. During those push-ups I subliminally send evil stink-eye thoughts my instructor's way, but unfortunately, when it's over, I feel strong and empowered. That makes it difficult to hate her. I do, however, think yoga would be more enjoyable if, instead of planks, we just rubbed our bellies chanting anti-fat ritual-like affirmations and then called it a day. But for now, I keep going.

My New Year's resolution for the coming year is to stop continually embarrassing myself. In the past, however, I've never been successful getting past the first week. Case in point recently, while grocery shopping, I placed an item in my cart that I had plucked off the shelf when I realized that my purse was gone. I panicked, thinking it was stolen, until I noticed that I also did not recognize many of the groceries. Gee... could it be because it WASN'T MY CART? A quick search and rescue mission found MY cart (with my purse) three aisles away—which goes to show you how much I pay attention (except when it comes to what you're wearing, of course!) A sweet elderly woman with the most perplexed look on her face was my unfortunate victim. One confession later and several minutes spent transferring three aisles-worth of my groceries out of her cart, I vowed to be more responsible next year. But I giggled as I remembered, *"Blessed is she who can laugh at herself for she will never cease to be entertained."*

Well, that's my year in review, dear friends. I hope your new year is an entertaining one as well.

Happy holidays,

Julie

Woman's Best Friend

*E*very family has a pet story. Unfortunately, mine does not cast me in a very favorable light, but it must be told.

In 1996, I took a sabbatical from work. I use the word sabbatical because it makes me sound smart and kind of teacher-ish. The truth of the matter is I just quit my job. One very hectic evening after leaving work, picking up my middle school-aged sons, then securing dinner via the McDonald's drive-through on our way to soccer practice, my son (age 10) asked me why I never smiled anymore.

So I quit; hence the sabbatical. The intent during that time was to commit myself fully to being the Kool-Aid Mom, which included getting my sons a dog. Every Kool-Aid Mom had a dog in the family, didn't she? The only problem was we didn't have a dog.

Enter Morgan, our beagle.

Now let me digress for a minute and say that although I grew up on a farm for the first nine years of my life, I never owned a dog. I agree. That is pretty unusual. Every farm has dogs, right? I'm pretty sure if you run through the entire rousing rendition of "Old McDonald had a Farm," there was a dog in the mix somewhere. But we never did. So Morgan was my first (and unfortunately only) experience living with someone from the animal kingdom, unless you count the fact that I raised one husband and two sons. If you're married and raised sons, you know that counts! Don't debate this one!

I was so excited about the prospect of being a "parent" again without having to suffer through swollen ankles and indigestion. I had visions of our beautiful beagle lying in front of a roaring fire on his tartan plaid bed, complete with a monogrammed name, `a la L.L. Bean, in our country home.

Morgan never uttered a sound for the first three days he came to live with us. Just imagine if you brought your newborn baby home from the hospital and he never cried. Would you not feel like you won the mother of all baby lotteries? Easy peasy! There were no late night whimperings, no barking, no growling. Nothing.

I later realized he was just toying with my emotions. Day four arrived and life in the Gaver household was never the same. Dogs (especially beagles) bark! I'm not saying he barked a lot but when you try to turn a hunting dog into a live-in-town kind of dog, there are bound to be repercussions. Every person who walked on the sidewalk in front of our house, across the street, or in the next block for that matter, received a Morgan-esque greeting.

Morgan was strong-willed. That does not bode well when the owner is a strong-willed redhead. So Morgan and I enrolled in obedience school, otherwise known as one more example of why I will NEVER be the Kool-Aid Mom. I still can't believe I was never called into the "principal's office" and asked if there was any chance we would be transferring to another school.

The other dogs learned obedience. Morgan's goal in life was to be Mr. Congeniality. Every week when we arrived for class, Morgan would survey the room and immediately roll over on his back and let the other dogs sample his, how should I say, kibbles and bits. I can emphatically assure you that he did NOT learn that from me! A friend of mine once told me that Morgan was merely demonstrating submissive behavior (a good thing in obedience training, apparently). To me, Morgan was a tart! Needless to say, I'm the one who learned something from obedience school. I learned that Morgan was easy, and also that he was the boss of me.

I like to think that I am a patient person, but for some reason, I was the most *impatient* person when I took Morgan out for his "morning constitutional." To this day, I still think he tarried just to show me who was in control. Had he asked for a newspaper before we'd head out on those cold winter mornings, I would have been better prepared for the lengthy stay, but noooooooooo. Once again, he toyed with my emotions by making me believe it would be quick trip. In retrospect, I realize I was probably being a tad unrealistic. How many people do *you* know who can poop on demand? These things take time. I can assure you that I did not potty train my two sons by standing over the top of them yelling, "Poop, dammit, poop!" That's just too much pressure for anyone, especially a dog!

How a 25-pound dog could drag a 125-pound woman up the street is still surprising to me. *(OK, 125 pounds might not be exactly the truth, but it sure looks good in print, so let's go with it, shall we?)* But that was when he was in hot pursuit of a squirrel, cat, groundhog, person, or leaf blowing in the wind. When he was tired, there was no negotiation. He would plop his butt on the sidewalk and refuse to budge, despite my pleas and cajoling. He'd wait until he had pushed my every last button (and then some), then make a detour onto someone's front yard and proceed to slide across their lawn on his behind. If I were telling this story in a speech perhaps I would attempt a demonstration, but then you would believe that Morgan DID learn some of his earlier mentioned whorish moves from his Master. But we loved Morgan in spite of his being such a petulant child.

Our first Christmas together was especially memorable. The tree lights were lit and the Christmas music was playing softly in the background. My husband, sons, and I were all seated in our traditional places and the morning gift exchange ritual had begun. Morgan lay peacefully in the room and it truly was like a scene from a Norman Rockwell painting. All of a sudden, my normally quiet, docile husband's eyes grew as large as saucers and he began to point at something across the room. He was speechless except for an odd sputtering, panting sound coming from his lips. We glanced across the room and at the same time heard my husband spew, "HE'S... he's... POOPING!!!!!!!!!!!!!!!!!!!!!!!!!!!!!!" On my beautiful country home braided rug. Oh yeah... NOW the dog can poop!

, , , , , , , , , , , , , , , , , , ,

The Rest
of the Story

After a lot of soul searching, we finally decided that Morgan would be happier living on the farm with my in-laws. There he could be, as they say in the self-help books, his true "authentic self." For many years we paid child support. We obviously had visitation rights since we spent a lot of time with my husband's family. It was the right choice for all of us and at the time of this printing, Morgan still goes to the barn every day with Pap to feed the animals (and poop). But I would be lying if I told you that I didn't feel twinges of guilt every time I see him. I was the "mother who abandoned her son." But in spite of it all, every time he sees me, he barks his beagle greeting and attempts to snuggle. Forgiveness is a wonderful thing, isn't it?

Your Mama
Raised
You Right

*O*ne day my son called to tell me about something that happened at his workplace. A female co-worker's boyfriend sent her a delivery consisting of *four* separate bouquets of roses. Each bouquet was a different color and contained a separate card. Upon seeing that all four arrangements were being delivered one at a time (to the *same* woman) and that the number of bouquets *coincidentally* corresponded with the number of words needed to individually spell out *will—you—marry—me?*, my son was convinced that he was going to witness his first marriage proposal. I love the fact that he has the emotional makeup to even think of something like that!

Unfortunately, the bouquets didn't equal a marriage proposal after all, but my son and I agreed that it would be an amazing way to pop the question (assuming the bouquets arrived in the proper sequence). I don't know the young man who sent the flowers but I DO know one thing about him... his mama definitely raised him right!

Speaking of romantic gestures, I witnessed the *mother* of grand gestures at my workplace many years ago. The husband of a coworker walked into her office one day, unannounced. When she looked up to see him standing there, he said,

"Get your purse. We have to go."

"Why? What's wrong?" she said with panic in her voice. *(That would rank right up there in my book with getting a phone call at 3 am. It can't be good!)*

"Because we have a flight for Hawaii that leaves in two hours." (Of course that was back in the day when you could actually get to the airport, check your luggage, go through security, go to the bathroom, and pick up a magazine and a box of Raisinettes before takeoff, all in less than two hours.)

"I can't go to Hawaii," Pat wailed, "I have to work." As if on cue, Pat's boss walked out of his adjacent office and said, "No, you don't. You're on vacation. You just didn't know it."

"But I've been scheduling appointments!" Once again the boss replied, "We've been rescheduling them for you behind your back."

She continued, "But what about the kids?" Her husband responded, "Mom's already at the house and the refrigerator is filled with food." Judging by the way the other women in the office began swarming to the scene, you'd think Brad Pitt was in the building. *(The rest of us were swooning by this time. Seriously, I was half expecting Mr. Wonderful to utter the words, "Here's looking at you, kid," or "You had me at hello." It just doesn't get much better than this... or does it???)*

"I can't!" she protested, "I have to go home and pack!" (What was *wrong* with this woman??? If that were me, surely by this time I would have thrown a tube of SPF 45 at him, saying, "Don't forget to get my back!")

His response? You'd better sit down for this one: "I've already packed for you and if I've forgotten anything or you don't like what I packed, just buy something new when we get there."

And off they went! Can you imagine what it was like for the poor husbands of the women who witnessed this fairy tale reenactment? I was peeling potatoes at the kitchen sink when Dan walked in that evening and innocently asked how my day went.

"WELL, you wouldn't believe what PAT'S husband did today!!!!" And before I finished the entire story (as I remembered it), it degraded into "I don't think you looooooveeee me. Why can't you be like Paaaaaat's husband???"

Poor guy. He never knew what hit 'em. And I'm guessing that Pat's hubby probably got snubbed by the rest of the men at the next company event.

Learning to
Love Yourself

*H*is name was Tad. In my very humble opinion, it was a rare and truly *exquisite* name for my very first crush! He was the most beautiful specimen of fifth grade masculinity that I had *ever* seen, and I was truly smitten! My crush on Tad constituted my first real awareness of the opposite sex other than being older sister and Queen Boss Lady to two younger brothers.

Being the young femme fatale that I was, I decided it was time to make my move. I mean, really, what little boy in his right mind WOULDN'T want me? And so, I did what any self-assured, assertive, hopeless romantic would do. I wrote him a note!

· ·

Do you like me? Please check one.

☐ Yes   ☐ No

· ·

During math class I mustered up the courage to give the note to my friend, who passed it to her friend, who passed it to Tad's friend, who then (after what seemed like an

ETERNITY) passed it to my Beloved.

Tad took one look at the note and said loudly (in the middle of a fascinating discussion on fractions), "Eeeeeuuuu-uwwwww! Her hair is ORANGE… and she has FRECKLES!!!!"

Apparently, having freckles ranked right up there with cooties, and we ALL know what a deal breaker that could be!

In hindsight, perhaps it was just a whisper, but in my devastated, highly impressionable mind it was as if Tad raced to the principal's office, grabbed the microphone exclusively used for the morning announcements, and announced to the WORLD that I was not only ugly, but a total LOSER.

How could this be? Wasn't Charlie Brown totally *infatuated* with the little red-headed girl? Wasn't he practically a *stalker*, loitering outside her house for hours hoping to capture a mere glimpse of this auburn-haired beauty? How could Tad diss the obvious characteristics that, until that moment, I *thought* made me special?

And thus began my lifelong journey, the same journey many

of us travel to sabotage our self-esteem based on information, not from our *inner voice*, but the opinions and attitudes of others.

Perhaps for you it was your height (too tall, too short), your weight (too heavy, too skinny), the way you talked, the length of your nose, the size of your ears, or some other ridiculously random characteristic that *someone else* arbitrarily decided was your weakness.

The time has come to move on! We women are *all* so very beautiful in unique and special ways. Embrace it! Love it! Own it!

So, on behalf of the new *Must Love Shoes* sisterhood, to all the "Tads" in the world, I say…

"Your Loss!"

. . . .

What Goes Around, Comes Around

*T*he saga continued. Mr. Not-So-Wonderful went to a different high school and a new cast of characters took the stage. I found myself as a teenager not only loathing my red hair and freckles, but the fact that I had not yet received my fair share from the Breast Fairy! I'd like to pretend that my reaction to all of this was "Quite frankly my dear, I don't give a damn," but, in reality, I did. And I was tired of waiting. *(To this day, I can't stand it when people are tardy, so consider yourselves forewarned)*

There were several adolescent boys in my grade who truly believed that their sole purpose in life was to call attention to me and others in the same situation. Their tactics were typical of prepubescent young men, but when you're hormonal, everything is blown out of proportion. In my mind, these boys were Satan's spawn (SS).

Once in geography, the teacher asked the class where the Flat Lands were located. A member of SS responded, "Julie's chest." Sometimes, if I was careless and happened to lock eyes with an SS, he would rub his palm over the surface of the desk (to symbolize flatness) and smirk. *Hater!*

Fast forward twenty years. I'm happy to report that the

Breast Fairy *did* finally make her highly anticipated appearance, but if you think you're over high school, try running into former classmates.

What goes around truly does comes around. Once I ran into one of the SS gang. How ironic it was that the boy who teased me so unmercifully for having no breasts had become a man who now had *no hair*!

Girls, I'd like to tell you that I took the high road during our chat. However, I must confess, that for some unexplainable reason, I continually had the most irresistible urge to rub… my… head.

You Can't
Tell Me
What to Do!

*A*s one of five children (and probably the bossiest), *"You can't tell me what to do!"* was a phrase I remember hearing (and saying) often. I'm guessing that if you are *half* as sassy and audacious as I think you are, you said it, too!

Even now, as grown women, when we sense that others (spouses, children, friends, co-workers, parents) try to define or manipulate us, our inner child's voice defiantly dispels the notion that we are not in control of our lives.

But how often have we limited our *own* capacities (even at an early age) without realizing it?

I recently began cleaning my attic. OK… it's been more like a demolition project. If you saw my attic, you would realize this is not a job for pansies. I've lived in the same house for 29 years and keep EVERYTHING! Hey! You never know when you're going to need that small black & white TV or the box from your first computer!

At any rate, I can tell you that this undertaking has been liberating and, at the same time, cathartic. Hidden under the eaves of the roof was an old, dusty, massive box that I recently began to explore. Inside were hundreds of school papers, pictures, and creative writing assignments from my elementary school years. Apparently it was gifted to *me* years ago when my mother was purging her attic *(and hopefully feeling liberated)*.

My first realization after perusing some of the papers was that I was a real suck-up! OK, maybe that was a little harsh! I was a pint-sized flaming-haired overachiever! Hmmmmm… I'm thinking that hasn't changed much because on the rare occasion I saw a paper with an 'S' on it, my adult self cringed just a little. (Back in my day, you didn't get A's and B's. You got S– Satisfactory, O– Outstanding, N– Needs Improvement).

There hidden among the treasures was a creative writing assignment in impeccably crafted cursive dated October 26, 1967. (I would have been 10 years old at the time—don't bother doing the math—I'm 52!). The title was "What Would I Like to Be When I Grow Up?" Here is the [unedited] version.

I would like very much to be an artist. Im' not very good at drawing but that's what I want to be. My library book this week is called "Art is Everywhere." The thing I can draw the best is scenery and animals. I have many

relatives that are artists. The reason is because I like to do arts and crafts.

Truthfully, my first thought was "Why didn't the teacher correct the placement of the apostrophe in the word 'I'm'? No *wonder* I still have issues today with punctuation!!!"

My second thought was, *"Why at the innocent age of ten did I think I was not a good artist?" Clearly the hundreds of pictures I pulled from the box did not support that self definition!"* OK, so the trees had these little snow cone-looking tops, and every single person's face looked strangely like that weird doll in the Chucky movies. And I will confess that in my self portraits, my right arm was clearly two feet longer than my left. Perhaps that was because I wanted to divert attention from the fact that, even at age 10, I clearly needed to draw a hairdo that didn't make me look like Bree VandeCamp in the first season of *Desperate Housewives.*

As I sat in my office with the contents of this pictorial walk down memory lane around me, I laughed out loud. At a very young age, I must have known that my future would not include entrance into the Chicago Art Institute. However, it was as if throughout my life I was inwardly saying, *"Listen here, Missy, you can't tell me what to do."*

Art has and will continue to be a vital part of my life. Although my vocation is not one of an artist, I have managed to find some semblance of *artistic expression* in all areas of my life: experimenting with new recipes, decorating my home, designing my gardens, crafting speeches, and enjoying the creative and expressive women who make up my circle of friends.

"I guess I showed her," I thought to myself as I hung the paper on the wall in my office. Whenever I find myself putting limitations on my potential, I glance at that assignment and reflect on the words of Vincent Van Gogh (who knew a thing or two about art):

> *"If you hear a voice within you saying,*
> *'You are not a painter,' then by all means paint....*
> *And that voice will be silenced."*

What about you, girlfriend? No one can tell you what you can or cannot do! Prove 'em wrong!

The Happy Game

*W*hen my sons were very young, they would occasionally wake in the middle of the night needing comfort or reassurance after a bad dream. As a parent, it is often difficult to find the right words when you've been roused from a deep sleep. *(I do believe we have a genetic predisposition to awake whenever a 5-year old is merely standing quietly by our beds staring into our sleeping faces. That is the only explanation why a mother wakes up sensing that her child is in the room when a father can sleep through an entire night of colicky screaming and not hear a thing!)*

At any rate, rational explanations for nightmares never seemed to assuage my sons' irrational fears. So, the *happy game* was born! We would alternate saying something that made us happy. It could be an activity we did together *(feeding the ducks, sled riding, visiting Grandma's, etc.)* or something that simply made us feel good *(often favorite foods made the list)*. As we alternatively listed each "happy thing," my son would smile and eventually the fears would subside. Before long, we were both in our "happy place" and asleep once again.

Occasionally now, I find myself feeling anxious over the complexities and stresses of living in today's world. For some reason, when we dwell on these things in the dark and stillness of the night, our problems seem much bigger than they are when viewed by the light of day. I've been known to play the happy game in my head while lying in bed hoping to resume much-needed sleep.

If you find yourself feeling unsettled or anxious, I invite *you* to play. When we reflect on the little things that add texture and fullness to our lives, we assume an attitude of gratitude, prayer, and mindfulness. What a blessing to simply reflect on sensory gifts that life offers. A greater awareness of these can take *us* to our happy place.

Make a list like I did. Start with the obvious (family, friends, health, etc.) but allow yourself to mosey on the page. Below are a few of my favorites.

The smell of the ground after it rains

Driving with the sun roof open on the first balmy spring night of the season

Comfort food
(too many to list but must include mashed potatoes and mac 'n cheese!)

Silly poems that rhyme

Long lunches with a friend

Soft, rich, beautiful fabrics

The smell of a burning logs in my fireplace

Naps

Small, cozy antique shops

Hardback books

Playdough, crayons and childhood things

The smell of a baby's head after his bath

Botanical gardens

Strangers who smile at me first

Long, hot bubble baths

Holding a warm cup of tea in my hands and
feeling the steam rise on my face

Stained glass windows

Porch swings and rocking chairs

The feeling of dirt in my hands

The fragrance of a hyacinth, lily, rose, and iris

Warm, bulky sweaters

Music so beautiful it makes me cry

Chocolate-covered cherries

' '

Be happy today!

' ' ' ' ' ' ' ' ' ' ' ' ' ' ' ' ' ' '

Finding
Your Voice

*S*everal years ago, my father was diagnosed with breast cancer. Though it strikes fewer than 1% of males, breast cancer is an illness that affects us all. A new case of breast cancer is diagnosed every three minutes. By the time you finish reading this book, you or someone you love could become a statistic. Have you ever noticed how little attention we pay to statistics until they knock on our door? Suddenly, the numbers become real and very personal.

Following a mastectomy, radiation and hormone treatment therapy, my dad is doing well. In addition, my personal journey has been filled with many close calls, biopsies, breast MRI's and benign lumpectomy surgery. As a consequence of these experiences, I am filled with gratitude to the vigilantes whose passion is finding a cure for this dreaded disease. They have found their voice and use it to bring attention to the importance of early detection and treatment.

The year following my dad's diagnosis and treatment, my sister and I walked in the Avon Walk for Breast Cancer in Washington, DC. As a professional speaker, I felt called to put down the microphone, pick up the sneakers and demonstrate the *"little less talk and a lot more action"* philosophy. Over two days we were able to raise $9,000 between the two of us and walked 39.3 miles as a way of giving back and paying tribute to our dad.

There were over 3,000 walkers and at least twice as many supporters lining the street throughout the two days. The hearts that beat beneath the sea of pink t-shirts were the hearts of our sisterhood: brave, fearless, audacious women who were joined through a common cause. Over the weekend, we shared tears of both joy and laughter. Humor really is the tie that binds us to one another and the messages on the walkers' and supporters' shirts said it best!

Do it for the ta-ta's.

Save 2nd base.

Rack attack!

One lump or two? None, please.

I'm a breast man.

The back of my shirt bore the names of 36 survivors and a few beautiful souls who fought their battles with grace and dignity. Although I didn't know some of them, I knew what they meant and continue to mean to the people who sponsored me. That kept me going when I wanted to quit. Only one name was written on the front of my shirt, over my heart: Dad.

I've always believed that the eyes are the window to the soul. At the 20-mile marker, I'm sure everyone could see that my soul was mostly exhausted. My feet hurt and I'd gotten very irritable. To add insult to injury, I had skipped the last bathroom stop, which was a *huge* mistake!

The streets were lined with cheering spectators shouting words of thanks and encouragement. As I glanced through the crowd looking for my family, my eyes were drawn to a bald and beautiful woman who looked to be in her mid-30's. She was standing along the curb. As our eyes met, she mouthed the words "thank you" to me. I cried and remembered why I was there.

As long as I live, I will never forget the final moments of this incredible two-day journey. As we rounded the final corner, I heard the roar of the crowd. There were *thousands* of people lining the streets which led us up the steps and into the Kennedy Center. A band played, and we walked through a massive sea of pink; people smiled, hugged, and patted us on the back as if they were waiting *just for us*. It felt so very humbling and extremely personal. My sister Nancy began to cry and I remember thinking, "This is what heaven will feel like." It brought new meaning to the word *homecoming*, and I will forever be changed because of it.

How about you, my friend? There is so much work to be done. Pick your cause. Find your voice. Take action. *If not you, then who?*

Rock-a-bye
Baby

A few years ago my husband and I became empty nesters. Our youngest son, Kevin, left for college. In spite of the fact that we had been planning for that day since Kevin was born, when it finally happened, we were not (emotionally) ready for the change.

Overnight, the phone stopped ringing. There was no more music blaring from the bedroom, no parade of teenagers raiding my cupboards and refrigerators at all hours. There were no shoes to pick up, no wet towels on the floor to fuss over. The house was empty and, to my dismay, I felt as if my heart was breaking.

I now silently cursed the many times during those tumultuous teenage years that I looked *forward* to this time! How quickly we, as parents, find ourselves wishing that we could turn back time. After Kevin's departure, I found myself walking into our *second* vacant bedroom and feeling very alone. And afraid.

One day a colleague called to see how I was handling the change. I replied that, in a very strange way, it felt as if someone had died. He responded by sharing a story that I will never forget and for which I will always be grateful.

In a small hospital room several years ago, Bill sat, with his brother-in-law Gene, next to his only sister and watched sadly as she quietly surrendered her fight against cancer. After she took her final breath, neither man moved to summon the nurse. They remained by her side, lost in quiet reflection over the woman they both loved.

At that moment, an old familiar tune began to play over the intercom system of the hospital. *Rock-a-bye Baby.* Its sweet melody filled the hallways and is played each time a baby is born at the hospital. The song is the hospital's way of announcing to patients and visitors that a new life has just entered the world.

"Listen to that," Gene murmured, breaking the silence. "One life has just ended and another has just begun."

Life is a series of deaths and rebirths, isn't it? Seasons come and go, and each brings new adventures and endless possibility. I look back on the early days of our empty nest now with an entirely different attitude, for I am not the same person I used to be, either. As my sons bravely ventured out into the world, I, too, took on new challenges with great hope and anticipation. I started growing my business, returned to school, and found courage to pursue goals for which I previously never had the time or courage.

For each of us, growth occurs at every age. Stay focused on the rebirth during every season in your life. *Rock-a-bye baby.*

*H*ave you ever noticed how everyone seems to have an Aunt Betty? Seriously, take an informal poll of all the people you know. Most will have an Aunt Betty to call their own. It's as if the Aunt Ruler of the world set out a decree that everyone would have an Aunt Betty in his or her life. I have three! Actually, that is my mother-in-law's name, too, so I really won the mother lode when it comes to Betties.

Carol is another popular aunt name. I have only one but she had such an impact on my life that I only needed one. Truthfully, she's my husband Dan's aunt, but I claim her as my own and she always introduced me to others as "her niece." Not her "nephew's wife," or her "niece-in-law," but her niece. That secretly always made me very proud.

During most of the time that I knew Carol, she lived with my in-laws. They had a unique living situation that worked for them. My husband and I benefited because there were three people living in that household who spoiled us, not just two.

Carol was a character in every sense of the word. She said what was on her mind. She never minced words, she was opinionated (especially when it came to politics), and, well... let me be totally honest... she could be very bossy. She didn't ask. She TOLD.

My mother-in-law, who was my children's day care provider, typically respected my wishes during my early, overprotective years of parenting. But not Carol. She fed the little darlings ice cream in spite of my 'no sugar' policy. When I objected, she'd simply reply, "ohhhhhh, it'll never hurt 'em," as she spoon-fed them homemade peach ice cream while aiding and abetting their first sugar high.

When they were young, she'd fix them their own cup of "coffee" to drink while she imbibed. Their concoction consisted of roughly two teaspoons of actual coffee; the remainder of the cup was filled with milk, giving their forbidden beverage a tawny, oh-so-grown-up appearance. She bought them cool sneakers with flashing lights in the heels and Tonka Trucks (the good kind made of metal, not plastic). Aunt Carol even let them play in her bedroom which, to a little boy, was no less magical than exploring a pirates cave chock full of inexpensive trinkets, glassware, and costume jewelry representing decades of *"what do we give Aunt Carol for her birthday?"* accumulation. She was a rare breed.

Most of what I know about flowers and gardening, I learned from Aunt Carol. She became the Rescue Mission for lost and hopeless plants. If a houseplant was dying, Carol adopted it temporarily, nursed it back to health, and returned it to you with stern instructions on its proper care and placement. She was a lover of the hibiscus, the Christmas cactus, and the fern. In the summer her porch overflowed with a vibrant mix of fuschia and purple hues along with a seemingly infinite supply of plastic pots bearing new start-ups from her endless plant divisions. At the end of each visit, she would shove a pot containing a few divided pieces of flora into your hands with a look that made you feel as if you had suddenly been entrusted with the crown jewel of the entire herbaceous world and that its survival depended solely on you!

Although Aunt Carol was considerably older than me, she demonstrated all the characteristics of a close friend. She never forgot my birthday, had a way of giving that perfect gift at Christmastime, and delighted in sharing special family recipes like Great Aunt Ruth's sticky buns and her coveted broccoli cheese casserole. She told me what most people never had the courage to say. Once, while listening to me lament the fact that I just couldn't drop any weight, Aunt Carol blurted, "You're not FAT!! Your legs are ALWAYS gonna be BIG 'cause that's just the way you're BUILT!" (Although a statement like that from my husband would earn him a free ticket to Lonely Island, Aunt Carol could get away with it.)

As Aunt Carol aged, she became increasingly quirky and unabashed about etiquette and what constituted proper decorum. She would share intimate details of her increasing health ailments with total strangers, wait until seated at the table in a restaurant to prepare her false teeth for insertion, and talk loudly about people when they were a mere two feet away. Her eccentricities, although embarrassing and frustrating at times, made her even more endearing and special to me. If only I could be less obsessed about what people think and as unapologetic about who I am! Carol lived her life fully and with great passion for the things she loved most: family, friends, flowers, food, and her beloved pets, which she had plenty of over the years.

I remember my last conversation with Aunt Carol. Her health declined gradually to the point where she required round-the-clock care. This became the dedicated task of my mother- and father-in-law. I climbed the steps to Aunt Carol's bedroom and stood above her hospital-like bed, leaning over so she could see my face and realize who was with her. We talked for only a short while and as I readied to leave, I leaned over and kissed her on the forehead. "I'll see you later this week," I whispered.

"No," she smiled sweetly back at me. *"I won't see you."*

She knew.

And she was ready.

It's odd. I didn't really cry much at Carol's funeral or even in the years since her death. When I'm gardening or in my kitchen, I often think of her. Her memory makes me smile and sometimes even laugh. She touched my life and taught me about so many things that add beauty and depth to my life. For that, I will always be grateful.

Funny....I'm crying now.

This Old House

I will always love an old house
for in those timbers strong
is love and life and memories
of children's carefree song.
A house that's used to wind and rain
with a towering oak above.
used to sunshine, laughter, lilacs
will protect those who give it love.

-Author Unknown

I, too, have always loved old houses. If you listen closely, they tell a story. Like the life lines that form on our faces with the passing years, old homes reveal the same kind of character. The older the house (and woman), the more fascinating the story.

My love story with our home began almost twenty-nine years ago when Dan and I walked through the front door of our mid-1800's federal style colonial home. It was the kind of place that made you feel warm and cozy inside, where you could put your feet on the furniture (even if you were company), a place where family and friends would want to gather at Christmastime. It had the heart and soul of Grandma's house; it made you feel safe, warm, and loved.

The previous owners, an elderly couple, had lived in the

house for over thirty years. It was obvious that our walk through the house together that last time was bittersweet for the Rices. As we entered each room, Mrs. Rice paused in the doorway, glancing around the room with a mixture of pride and sadness. She shared beautiful, poignant stories about the Rice's lives and how she felt about raising her family in what was soon to become *our* old house. At that moment I realized that I had just received a valuable piece of history, accompanied by a newfound sense of duty and responsibility to continue a tradition of loving care. We were up for the challenge.

Having now raised two sons in this old house, I can already understand the emotion Mrs. Rice felt that last day when she relinquished the keys. As is true for most families, we had a traditional spot in the back yard where every first day of school photo was taken. I will always treasure the laughter and conversation which flowed easily from my kitchen during family dinners and gatherings. I remember the squeak of the old wooden back door announcing Dan's arrival after a long day's work. I learned how to gingerly tiptoe across the antiquated wide wood plank floors in my babies' bedrooms so as not to awaken them while they slept. I will always picture my 6'1" "baby" ducking to avoid hitting his head on the hall doorway which was constructed when people were obviously much shorter. The weathered marble stone at the front and back doors is evidence that many people, both residents and guests, have passed through this place I've called home.

This past summer a serendipitous thing happened. Out of the blue, I received a phone call from a woman named Audrey who was in her 70's and now lives in North Carolina. She explained that she visits Maryland on occasion because her family still lives in the area. Her aunt and uncle were one of the previous owners of our home and she spent many memorable childhood years there. It was as if an old friend had called. Without even so much as a lull in the conversation, we talked easily about our home and how she had always longed to return. The inevitable question was eventually asked: "Could I bring my family to see your home during my next visit north?" There was only one possible answer: yes! I felt an immediate connection to this likeable woman and was excited about the prospect of seeing our home through her eyes.

Our visit was delightful and as she and her family readied to leave, we discussed the possibility of her gathering her two cousins, Julia and Patsy, the cousin who actually lived in my house, for an encore "house reunion."

Several weeks later, the four of us met. As we walked throughout the house and property, it felt almost surreal. I had never met these women and yet, at the same time, I felt as if I had known them forever. Watching their faces as they laughed, reminisced, and shared heartfelt stories about their families and loved ones in my home made me realize that this old house had now become the tie that would forever bind us together. Audrey's mother was proposed to in the "parlor" (which is now my living room). Julia's mother planted the maple seedlings which are now towering trees that shade my house. Patsy revealed that one of our outbuildings housed a healthy collection of chickens which she cared for. Old photos provided authenticity to many of the suspicions I had about how the house and property evolved throughout the years.

Their stories have now become part of mine. Someday another young couple will cross the weathered marble of our front doorstep and they, too, will fall in love. And when that time comes, I will pass it on, as so many others have before me. And I imagine that I, too, will pause, reflect, and share *my love and life and memories*, because that is what old houses are for.

*Y*es, there IS magic in a gorgeous pair of shoes. Just ask Dorothy from the *Wizard of Oz*. That girl truly understands the power of a pair of smokin' red pumps.

The Wizard of Oz was my favorite movie as a young girl. Not only did I love those shoes, but I loved the Scarecrow, Tin Man, and Lion. These lovable characters searched for what they thought they lacked, only to learn that it was already hidden deep within. They just needed someone to help them discover the gift.

And so it is with each of us. When will we ever learn that if we follow that "yellow brick road" into the deep recesses of our spirit, we discover that we, too, have enormous gifts and power? Our brains, heart, and courage are what make women so spectacular!

As I reflect on my life, I realize there have been many who have taught, counseled, inspired, and loved me. But three women in particular will always hold a special place in my heart for teaching me the true meaning of having brains, heart, and courage.

Nancy, my "scarecrow," managed the small office where I

worked in the early 80's. Unable to find a job in my field of study, I took a position that offered little challenge and promise of a career path. Nancy taught me the importance of professional development and the value of continuing education. While working full-time, Nancy earned her MBA, attending classes in the evenings, and eventually completed a doctorate program in her field of study. Even now, she is constantly reading, growing, and encouraging others to pursue excellence through the acquisition of knowledge. Nancy's attitude inspires me to continue exercising my brain and to learn more, do more, and be more.

Barry is my "tin man." She epitomizes Christian faith in action and pours her heart into serving others. With great humility, she gives her time, energy, resources, and talent toward helping those who are hungry, homeless, and in need of hope. Barry sees your potential even when you've given up on yourself. More importantly, she unapologetically wears her heart on her sleeve, speaking passionately to others about the need to walk the servant talk. She makes me want to be a better person.

Finally, there is a "lion" in my life who has shown me the true meaning of courage. Bravery does not always roar. For this strong woman, bravery showed up in the quiet hours of the morning many years ago when she took her first courageous step toward ending her addiction to alcohol. Watching her journey of sobriety has taught me the true meaning of "one day at a time." Whenever I am afraid, I think of the valor this woman demonstrates every day of her recovery. I am filled with hope and confidence knowing that I, too, can face any hardship life hands me with the same tenacity.

Brains, heart, and courage. What a blessing it is to know women like these in our lives. As our time together comes to an end, I challenge you to reflect on the women in *your* life who have inspired you, whose influence has helped to make you who you are today.

But I imagine, though, that if you were completely honest, you would realize that you, too, possess these magnificent traits. You've got brains, heart, and courage. Embrace them. Celebrate the woman you are! In the words of Glenda, the good witch:

> You've always had the power, my dear.
> You've had it all along.

· · · · · · · · · · · · · · · · · ·

Linda Hull

from

Paula Hatch   May 6, 2011